Life is Simple

EVERY MOMENT MATTERS

PARACLETE PRESS
BREWSTER, MASSACHUSETTS

2017 First Printing

Life Is Simple: Every Moment Matters

Copyright © 2017 by Paraclete Press, Inc.

ISBN 978-1-61261-928-6

Library of Congress Cataloging-in-Publication Data:

Names: Paraclete Press.
Title: Life is simple : every moment matters.
Description: Brewster, Massachusetts : Paraclete Press, 2017.
Identifiers: LCCN 2017006354 | ISBN 9781612619286 (hardcover)
Subjects: LCSH: Life--Quotations, maxims, etc.
Classification: LCC BD431 .L4185 2017 | DDC 248.4--dc23
LC record available at https://lccn.loc.gov/2017006354

10 9 8 7 6 5 4 3 2 1

Published by Paraclete Press Brewster, Massachusetts
www.paracletepress.com

Printed in the United States of America

Contents

Introduction

Life today is hectic, busy, and complicated—full of anxiety-producing news and other things that trigger our fight-or-flight instinct even though we're not in any real danger. It wears on our nerves. The antidote has been shared by great sages and saints throughout the ages and across the spiritual traditions: live in the present, not the past or future; be grateful for what you have; appreciate the little things; cultivate greater awareness of the world and people around you; don't be dragged down by anxiety or remorse; never go to bed angry; cultivate serenity and receptivity; generate kindness and love toward everything around you.

In response to our frenetic world, many people today are seeking greater simplicity, looking to make their lives calmer and more grounded. They're connecting with nature, and more and more, they're making lifestyle choices like slow food and cutting the cable. And especially, they're turning to spiritual answers from the older traditions.

What follows is a cross-section of expressions of the related themes of simplicity and living in the present moment. There are sayings, prayers, poems, hymns, and some extended passages. Each may offer you a new insight or a needed reminder—a little nudge to keep it simple, be here now, appreciate what surrounds you, and walk gently through this life. Dip into this collection to start your day, end your day, or whenever you need a little bit of calm.

Great Thoughts on Simplicity and the Present Moment

I am convinced, both by faith and experience, that to maintain one's self on this earth is not a hardship but a pastime, if we will live simply and wisely.
—HENRY DAVID THOREAU

Nothing is more highly to be prized than the value of each day.
—JOHANN WOLFGANG VON GOETHE,
maxim 332 in *Maxims and Reflections*

If we cling to our idea of hope in the future, we might not notice the peace and joy that are available in the present moment. The best way to take care of the future is to take care of the present moment.
—THICH NHAT HANH,
in *Living Buddha, Living Christ*

It is not knowing much, but realizing and relishing things
interiorly, that contents and satisfies the soul.

—ST. IGNATIUS

The revelation that we have everything we need in life to
make us happy but simply lack the conscious awareness to
appreciate it can be as refreshing as lemonade on a hot after-
noon. Or it can be as startling as cold water being thrown in
our face. How many of us go through our days parched and
empty, thirsting after happiness, when we're really standing
knee-deep in the river of abundance?

—SARAH BAN BREATHNACH
Simple Abundance: A Daybook of Comfort and Joy

True progress does not consist in a multitude of self-searching,
or of austerities, troubles, and strife. It means simply to will
nothing of self and everything of God, cheerfully performing
each day's round as God appoints it for us, seeking nothing,
refusing nothing, finding everything in the present moment,

*and allowing God, who does everything, to do his pleasure in
and by us without the slightest resistance on our part.
Oh, how happy is the person who has attained this state!
How full of good things is that soul, when it appears to be
emptied of everything!*

—FRANÇOIS FÉNELON
"Meeting Temptations," *The Complete Fénelon*

*We still cultivate that sense of awareness of what the
clientele needs—despite the trends, despite the fashion. Our
dishes are still relatively simple, focusing on the deep, true
flavors rather than elaborate presentations.*

—ERIC RIPERT (CHEF),
On the Line: Inside the World of Le Bernardin

There is more to life than increasing its speed.

—MAHATMA GANDHI

*When I have made the journey to my true self, or even
glimpsed it and want to live my life from that center,
I relate to others in a new way. For one thing, out of my
silence I really hear their words–hear their words. I
have to be silent to listen and inwardly quiet to be fully
present to another, to hear another's word, especially if
I would hear its full import. How often have I engaged
in conversations where I am not really hearing the other
because my own words are muscling their way into
expression, and I have ears only for my own words? And if I
am not attentive enough, silent enough to hear their words,
I don't catch their nonverbal messages either.*

—SISTER JEREMY HALL, OSB,
from *Silence, Solitude, Simplicity: A Hermit's Love Affair
with a Noisy, Crowded, and Complicated World*

*We all look for happiness, but without knowing where
to find it: like drunkards who look for their house,
knowing dimly that they have one.*

—VOLTAIRE

You are accepted. You are accepted, accepted by that which is greater than you, and the name of which you do not know. Do not ask for the name now; perhaps you will find it later. Do not try to do anything now; perhaps later you will do much. Do not seek for anything; do not perform anything; do not intend anything. Simply accept the fact that you are accepted!

—PAUL TILLICH

He who works with his hands is a laborer.
He who works with his hands and his head is a craftsman.
He who works with his hands and his head and
his heart is an artist.

—AUTHOR UNKNOWN
(sometimes incorrectly attributed to St. Francis or Louis Nizer)

Peace comes from not needing to control everything and not needing to have everything and not needing to surpass everyone and not needing to know everything and not needing to have everyone else be like me.

—JOAN CHITTISTER, OSB,
Wisdom Distilled from the Daily

Before enlightenment, chop wood and carry water;
After enlightenment, chop wood and carry water.

—ZEN PROVERB

If you want to know what it means to be happy, look at a flower, a bird, a child; they are perfect images of the kingdom. For they live from moment to moment in the eternal now with no past and no future.

—ANTHONY DE MELLO, SJ

*Shibui describes a profound, unassuming, quiet feeling.
It is unobtrusive and unostentatious. It may have hidden
attainments, but they are not paraded or displayed.
The form is simple and must have been arrived at with
an economy of means. Shibui is never complicated or
contrived. . . . Shibui beauty, as in the beauty of the tea
ceremony, is beauty that makes an artist of the viewer.*
—ELIZABETH GORDON,
editor-in-chief of *House Beautiful*, in the August 1960 issue

*Of course reading and thinking are important but, my God,
food is important too. How fortunate we are to be food-
consuming animals. Every meal should be a treat and one
ought to bless every day which brings with it a good digestion
and the precious gift of hunger.*
—IRIS MURDOCH, *The Sea, the Sea*

*Nature's simplicity hides a greater complexity than man's.
Beauty requires neither indirectness nor intricacy. Try to
add or contrive, and life vanishes. Great detail and high*

finish have to do with technique but have nothing to do directly with beauty. In fact, they interfere with it. Lovely things are almost always simply made.

—SOETSU YANAGI
on art, in *The Unknown Craftsman*,
translated by Bernard Leach

If you are waiting for anything in order to live and love without holding back, then you suffer. Every moment is the most important moment of your life. No future time is better than now to let down your guard and love.

—DAVID DEIDA

Being Present in the Bible

Whatever you do, do from the heart, as for the Lord and not for others.

COLOSSIANS 3:23 (NABRE)

You see, my heart overflowed with bitterness *and cynicism*;
  I felt as if someone stabbed me in the back.
But I didn't know *the truth*;
  I have been acting like a stupid animal toward You.
But *look at this*: You are still holding my right hand;
  You have been all along.

PSALM 73:21-23 (VOICE)

Rejoice in the Lord always; again I will say, Rejoice. Let your gentleness be known to everyone. The Lord is near. Do not worry about anything, but in everything by prayer and supplication with thanksgiving let your requests be made known to God. And the peace of God, which surpasses all understanding, will guard your hearts and your minds in Christ Jesus.

Finally, beloved, whatever is true, whatever is honorable, whatever is just, whatever is pure, whatever is pleasing, whatever is commendable, if there is any excellence and if there is anything worthy of praise, think about these

15

things. Keep on doing the things that you have learned and received and heard and seen in me, and the God of peace will be with you.

PHILIPPIANS 4:4–9 (NRSV)

Build houses and make yourselves at home. Put in gardens and eat what grows in that country. Marry and have children. Encourage your children to marry and have children so that you'll thrive in that country and not waste away. Make yourselves at home there and work for the country's welfare.

JEREMIAH 29:5–7 (MSG)

My heart is not proud, LORD,
   my eyes are not haughty;
I do not concern myself with great matters
   or things too wonderful for me.
But I have calmed and quieted myself,
   I am like a weaned child with its mother;
   like a weaned child I am content.

Israel, put your hope in the LORD
   both now and forevermore.

PSALM 131 (NIV)

"I tell you not to worry about everyday life—whether you have enough food and drink, or enough clothes to wear. Isn't life more than food, and your body more than clothing? Look at the birds. They don't plant or harvest or store food in barns, for your heavenly Father feeds them. And aren't you far more valuable to him than they are? Can all your worries add a single moment to your life?

"And why worry about your clothing? Look at the lilies of the field and how they grow. They don't work or make their clothing, yet Solomon in all his glory was not dressed as beautifully as they are. And if God cares so wonderfully for wildflowers that are here today and thrown into the fire tomorrow, he will certainly care for you. Why do you have so little faith?

"So don't worry about these things, saying, 'What will we eat? What will we drink? What will we wear?' These things dominate the thoughts of unbelievers, but your heavenly Father already knows all your needs. Seek the Kingdom of God above all else, and live righteously, and he will give you everything you need.

"So don't worry about tomorrow, for tomorrow will bring its own worries. Today's trouble is enough for today."

—MATTHEW 6:25B–34 (NLT)

Poems and Songs

"The pedigree of honey"

EMILY DICKINSON

The pedigree of honey
Does not concern the bee;
A clover, any time, to him
Is aristocracy.

"The Daffodils"

WILLIAM WORDSWORTH

I wandered lonely as a cloud
That floats on high o'er vales and hills,
When all at once I saw a crowd,
A host, of golden daffodils;
Beside the lake, beneath the trees,
Fluttering and dancing in the breeze.

Continuous as the stars that shine
And twinkle on the milky way,
They stretched in never-ending line
Along the margin of a bay:
Ten thousand saw I at a glance,
Tossing their heads in sprightly dance.

The waves beside them danced; but they
Out-did the sparkling waves in glee:
A poet could not but be gay,
In such a jocund company:

I gazed—and gazed—but little thought
What wealth the show to me had brought:

For oft, when on my couch I lie
In vacant or in pensive mood,
They flash upon that inward eye
Which is the bliss of solitude;
And then my heart with pleasure fills,
And dances with the daffodils.

"Simple Gifts"

ELDER JOSEPH BRACKETT

"Simple Gifts" is part of the American DNA. The hymn was composed in 1848 by Elder Joseph Brackett (1797–1882), who lived in a Shaker community in Gotham, Maine. Elder Brackett was fifty-one when he composed "Simple Gifts," which has endured for over 160 years. The song rocketed into popular consciousness when twentieth-century American composer Aaron Copland incorporated it into the Martha Graham ballet he scored called *Appalachian Spring*. "Simple Gifts" is a dance song. Unlike many New England Protestants, Shakers loved to dance. They saw dance not as a dangerous secular temptation, but as a sacred act—a way to get closer to the divine. "Simple Gifts" never uses the word *dance*, but in the 1960s, English lyricist Sydney Carter wrote new words blending mystical imagery, a message about Jesus, and his idea of the Shaker sensibility to the melody of "Simple Gifts," and created the immensely popular hymn "Lord of the Dance."

Here is the original Shaker version:

'Tis the gift to be simple, 'tis the gift to be free
   'Tis the gift to come down where we ought to be,
And when we find ourselves in the place just right,
   'Twill be in the valley of love and delight.
When true simplicity is gained,
   To bow and to bend we shan't be ashamed,
To turn, turn will be our delight,
   Till by turning, turning we come 'round right.

"My Kingdom"

LOUISA MAY ALCOTT

A little kingdom I possess,
Where thoughts and feelings dwell,
And very hard I find the task
Of governing it well;
For passion tempts and troubles me,
A wayward will misleads,
And selfishness its shadow casts,
On all my will and deeds.

How can I learn to rule myself,
To be the child I should,
Honest and brave, nor ever tire
Of trying to be good?
How can I keep a sunny soul
To shine along life's way?
How can I tune my little heart,
To sweetly sing all day?

Dear Father, help me with the love
That castest out my fear!
Teach me to lean on Thee and feel
That thou art very near.
That no temptation is unseen,
No childish grief too small,
Since Thou, with patience infinite,
Dost soothe and comfort all.

I do not ask for any crown
But that which all may win;
Nor try to conquer any world
Except the one within.
Be Thou my Guide until I find,
Led by a tender hand,
Thy happy kingdom in myself
And dare to take command.

"The Elixir"

GEORGE HERBERT

Teach me, my God and King,
    In all things Thee to see,
And what I do in anything
    To do it as for Thee.

    Not rudely, as a beast,
    To run into an action;
But still to make Thee prepossest,
    And give it his perfection.

    A man that looks on glass,
    On it may stay his eye;
Or if he pleaseth, through it pass,
    And then the heav'n espy.

All may of Thee partake:
Nothing can be so mean,
Which with his tincture—"for Thy sake"—
Will not grow bright and clean.

A servant with this clause
Makes drudgery divine:
Who sweeps a room as for Thy laws,
Makes that and th' action fine.

This is the famous stone
That turneth all to gold;
For that which God doth touch and own
Cannot for less be told.

"Desiderata"

MAX EHRMANN

Go placidly amid the noise and the haste, and remember what peace there may be in silence. As far as possible, without surrender, be on good terms with all persons.

Speak your truth quietly and clearly; and listen to others, even to the dull and the ignorant; they too have their story.

Avoid loud and aggressive persons; they are vexatious to the spirit. If you compare yourself with others, you may become vain or bitter, for always there will be greater and lesser persons than yourself.

Enjoy your achievements as well as your plans. Keep interested in your own career, however humble; it is a real possession in the changing fortunes of time.

Exercise caution in your business affairs, for the world is full of trickery. But let this not blind you to what virtue there is; many persons strive for high ideals, and everywhere life is full of heroism.

Be yourself. Especially, do not feign affection. Neither be cynical about love; for in the face of all aridity and disenchantment it is as perennial as the grass.

Take kindly the counsel of the years, gracefully surrendering the things of youth.

Nurture strength of spirit to shield you in sudden misfortune. But do not distress yourself with dark imaginings. Many fears are born of fatigue and loneliness.

Beyond a wholesome discipline, be gentle with yourself. You are a child of the universe no less than the trees and the stars; you have a right to be here.

And whether or not it is clear to you, no doubt the universe is unfolding as it should. Therefore be at peace with God, whatever you conceive Him to be.

And whatever your labors and aspirations, in the noisy confusion of life, keep peace in your soul. With all its sham, drudgery and broken dreams, it is still a beautiful world. Be cheerful. Strive to be happy.

"My Symphony"

WILLIAM ELLERY CHANNING

To live content with small means.

To seek elegance rather than luxury,

and refinement rather than fashion.

To be worthy not respectable,

and wealthy not rich.

To study hard, think quietly, talk gently,

act frankly, to listen to stars, birds, babes,

and sages with open heart, to bear all cheerfully,

do all bravely, await occasions, hurry never.

In a word, to let the spiritual,

unbidden and unconscious,

grow up through the common.

This is to be my symphony.

Two Wings to Soar Above the Earth

from *The Imitation of Christ*

THOMAS À KEMPIS

S implicity and purity are the two wings with which a person soars above the earth and all temporary nature. Simplicity is in the intention, purity in the affection: Simplicity turns to God; purity unites with and enjoys God.

No good action will be difficult and painful if you are free from uncontrolled desires; when the one simple intention of your mind is to obey the will of God and do good to your fellow creatures, you will enjoy this internal freedom.

If your heart is rightly disposed, every creature will be a book of divine knowledge; a mirror of life in which you might contemplate the eternal power and generosity of the author of life; for there is no creature, however small and abject, that does not reflect the goodness of God.

Such is the universe of the spirit; such is its perception and judgment of outward things. If you have simplicity and purity, you will be able to comprehend all things clearly, and behold them without danger: the pure heart safely travels through not only heaven, but hell.

I don't think anyone "finds" joy

from *I Will Not Die an Unlived Life*

DAWNA MARKOVA

Who am I when I am no longer doing, no longer productive, no longer indispensable to so many others? I have to pay attention to my own attention: Where does it go, to whom, and why? Is it really possible to give all of it to one thing at a time?

I need a kind of spiritual inhalation, a spaciousness that comes when I am living from the inside out. Only in this way can I find my joy again, the tenderness I can feel toward myself and the world. *Find* is the wrong word. I don't think anyone "finds" joy. Rather, we cultivate it by searching for the preciousness of small things, the ordinary miracles, that strengthen our hearts so we can keep them open to what is difficult: delight in taking a shower or a slow walk that has no destination, in touching something soft, in noticing the one small, black bird who sings every morning from the top of the big old pine tree that guards this cabin. I need to give my attention to the simple things that give me pleasure with the same fervor I have been giving it to the complex things with which I drive myself crazy.

Touching Deeply the Present Moment

from *Living Buddha, Living Christ*

THICH NHAT HANH

The Buddha was asked, "Sir, what do you and your monks practice?" he replied, "We sit, we walk, and we eat." The questioner continued, "But sir, everyone sits, walks, and eats," and the Buddha told him, "When we sit, we know we are sitting. When we walk, we know we are walking. When we eat, we know we are eating." Most of the time, we are lost in the past or carried away by future projects and concerns. When we are mindful, touching deeply the present moment, we can see and listen deeply, and the fruit are always understanding, acceptance, love, and the desire to relieve suffering and bring joy. When our beautiful child comes up to us and smiles, we are completely there for her.

I Was Something That Lay Under the Sun and Felt It

from *My Ántonia*

WILLA CATHER

I can remember exactly how the country looked to me as I walked beside my grandmother along the faint wagon-tracks on that early September morning. Perhaps the glide of long railway travel was still with me, for more than anything else I felt motion in the landscape; in the fresh, easy-blowing morning wind, and in the earth itself, as if the shaggy grass were a sort of loose hide, and underneath it herds of wild buffalo were galloping, galloping. . . .

Alone, I should never have found the garden—except, perhaps, for the big yellow pumpkins that lay about unprotected by their withering vines—and I felt very little interest in it when I got there. I wanted to walk straight on through the red grass and over the edge of the world, which could not be very far away. The light air about me told me that the world ended here: only the ground and sun and sky were left, and if one went a little farther there would be only sun and sky, and one would float off into them, like the tawny hawks which sailed over our heads making slow shadows on the grass. While grandmother took the pitchfork we found standing in one of the rows and dug potatoes, while I picked them up out of the soft brown earth and put them into the bag, I kept looking up at the hawks that were doing what I might so easily do.

When grandmother was ready to go, I said I would like to stay up there in the garden awhile.

She peered down at me from under her sunbonnet. "Aren't you afraid of snakes?"

"A little," I admitted, "but I'd like to stay, anyhow."

"Well, if you see one, don't have anything to do with him. The big yellow and brown ones won't hurt you; they're bull-snakes and help to keep the gophers down. Don't be scared if you see anything look out of that hole in the bank over there. That's a badger hole. He's about as big as a big 'possum, and his face is striped, black and white. He takes a chicken once in a while, but I won't let the men harm him. In a new country a body feels friendly to the animals. I like to have him come out and watch me when I'm at work."

Grandmother swung the bag of potatoes over her shoulder and went down the path, leaning forward a little. The road followed the windings of the draw; when she came to the first bend, she waved at me and disappeared. I was left alone with this new feeling of lightness and content.

I sat down in the middle of the garden, where snakes could scarcely approach unseen, and leaned my back against a warm yellow pumpkin. There were some ground-cherry bushes growing along the furrows, full of fruit. I turned back the papery triangular sheaths that protected the berries and ate a few. All about me giant grasshoppers, twice as big as any I had ever seen, were doing acrobatic feats among the dried vines. The gophers scurried up and down the ploughed ground. There in the sheltered draw-bottom the wind did not blow very hard, but I could hear it singing its humming tune up on the level, and I could see the tall grasses wave. The earth was warm under me, and warm as I crumbled it through my fingers. Queer little red bugs came out and moved in slow squadrons around me. Their backs were polished vermilion, with black spots. I kept as still as I could. Nothing happened. I did not expect anything to happen. I was something that lay under the sun and felt it, like the pumpkins, and I did not want to be anything more. I was entirely happy. Perhaps we feel like that when we die and become a part of something entire, whether it is sun and air, or goodness and knowledge. At any rate, that is happiness; to be dissolved into something complete and great. When it comes to one, it comes as naturally as sleep.

Simplicity with a Capital "S"

from *The Natural House*

FRANK LLOYD WRIGHT

As we live and as we are, Simplicity—with a capital "S"—is difficult to comprehend nowadays. We are no longer truly simple. We no longer live in simple terms or places. Life is a more complex struggle now. It is now valiant to be simple: a courageous thing to even want to be simple. It is a spiritual thing to comprehend what simplicity means.

Stay Present to What You're Seeing

from *Centering Prayer and Inner Awakening*

THE REV. DR. CYNTHIA BOURGEAULT

With practice you may be able to notice when your buttons are being pushed or you find yourself slipping into self-pity or self-righteousness, but noticing it doesn't necessarily make the mood shift. Sometimes the very best you can do is to stay present to what you're seeing, including enduring the gap in yourself between seeing and being able to do. . . . But no conscious seeing is ever wasted. If all you can do is wave goodbye to yourself as you go over the waterfall, this is a billion times more important than changing anything. Seeing creates a new relationship within yourself, and eventually that new relationship will bear fruit in the power to do. But doing is never the point. Every seeing, no matter how calamitous to the ego, is an enhancement of Being, a strengthening of the connection of the worlds within you. If you keep these points in mind, you will begin to develop a whole new way of living within yourself, and your life will change.

The Wood-Road Was Not a Place for Common Noisy Conversation

from *The Country of the Pointed Firs*

SARAH ORNE JEWETT

William led the way across the pasture, and I followed with a deep sense of pleased anticipation. I do not believe that my companion had expected me to make any objection, but I knew that he was gratified by the easy way that his plans for the day were being seconded. He gave a look at the sky to see if there were any portents, but the sky was frankly blue; even the doubtful morning haze had disappeared.

We went northward along a rough, clayey road, across a bare-looking, sunburnt country full of tiresome long slopes where the sun was hot and bright, and I could not help observing the forlorn look of the farms. There was a great deal of pasture, but it looked deserted, and I wondered afresh why the people did not raise more sheep when that seemed the only possible use to make of their land. I said so to Mr. Blackett, who gave me a look of pleased surprise.

"That's what she always maintains," he said eagerly. "She's right about it, too; well, you'll see!" I was glad to find myself approved, but I had not the least idea whom he meant, and waited until he felt like speaking again.

A few minutes later we drove down a steep hill and entered a large tract of dark spruce woods. It was delightful to be sheltered from the afternoon sun, and when we had gone some distance in the shade, to my great pleasure William turned the horse's head toward some bars, which he let down, and I drove through into one of those narrow, still, sweet-scented by-ways which seem to be paths rather than roads. Often we had to put aside the heavy drooping branches which barred the way, and once, when a sharp twig struck William in the face, he announced with such spirit that somebody ought to go through there with an axe, that I felt unexpectedly guilty.

So far as I now remember, this was William's only remark all the way through the woods to Thankful Hight's folks, but from time to time he pointed or nodded at something which I might have missed: a sleepy little owl snuggled into the bend of a branch, or a tall stalk of cardinal flowers where the sunlight came down at the edge of a small, bright piece of marsh. Many times, being used to the company of Mrs. Todd and other friends who were in the habit of talking, I came near making an idle remark to William, but I was for the most part happily preserved; to be with him only for a short time was to live on a different level, where thoughts served best because they were thoughts in common; the primary effect upon our minds of the simple things and beauties that we saw.

Once when I caught sight of a lovely gay pigeon-woodpecker eyeing us curiously from a dead branch, and instinctively turned toward William, he gave an indulgent, comprehending nod which silenced me all the rest of the way. The wood-road was not a place for common noisy conversation; one would interrupt the birds and all the still little beasts that belonged there. But it was mortifying to find how strong the habit of idle speech may become in one's self. One need not always be saying something in this noisy world.

To Know How to Be Ready

from *Amiel's Journal*

HENRI-FRÉDÉRIC AMIEL

15th August 1851. — To know how to be ready, a great thing, a precious gift, and one that implies calculation, grasp and decision. To be always ready a man must be able to cut a knot, for everything cannot be untied; he must know how to disengage what is essential from the detail in which it is enwrapped, for everything cannot be equally considered; in a word, he must be able to simplify his duties, his business, and his life. To know how to be ready, is to know how to start.

It is astonishing how all of us are generally cumbered up with the thousand and one hindrances and duties which are not such, but which nevertheless wind us about with their spider threads and fetter the movement of our wings. It is the lack of order which makes us slaves; the confusion of to-day discounts the freedom of to-morrow.

Confusion is the enemy of all comfort, and confusion is born of procrastination. To know how to be ready we must be able to finish. Nothing is done but what is finished. The things which we leave dragging behind us will start up again later on before us and harass our path. Let each day take thought for what concerns it, liquidate its own affairs and respect the day which is to follow, and then we shall be always ready. To know how to be ready is at bottom to know how to die.

7th September 1851 (Aix). — It is ten o'clock at night. A strange and mystic moonlight, with a fresh breeze and a sky crossed by a few wandering clouds, makes our terrace delightful. These pale and gentle rays shed from the zenith a subdued and penetrating peace; it is like the calm joy or the pensive smile of experience, combined with a certain stoic strength. The stars shine, the leaves tremble in the silver light. Not a sound in all the landscape; great gulfs of shadow under the green alleys and at the corners of the steps. Everything is secret, solemn, mysterious.

O night hours, hours of silence and solitude!—with you are grace and melancholy; you sadden and you console. You speak to us of all that has passed away, and of all that must still die, but you say to us, "Courage!"—and you promise us rest.

2d April 1852. — What a lovely walk! Sky clear, sun rising, all the tints bright, all the outlines sharp, save for the soft and misty infinite of the lake. A pinch of white frost powdered the fields, lending a metallic relief to the hedges of green box, and to the whole landscape—still without leaves—an air of health and vigor, of youth and freshness. "Bathe, disciple, thy thirsty soul in the dew of the dawn!" says Faust to us and he is right. The morning air breathes a new and laughing energy into veins and marrow. If every day is a repetition of life, every dawn signs as it were a new contract with existence.

At dawn everything is fresh, light, simple, as it is for children. At dawn spiritual truth, like the atmosphere, is more transparent, and our organs, like the young leaves, drink in the light more eagerly, breathe in more ether, and less of things earthly. If night and the starry sky speak to the meditative soul of God, of eternity and the infinite, the dawn is the time for projects, for resolutions, for the birth of action. While the silence and the "sad serenity of the azure vault" incline the soul to self-recollection, the vigor and gaiety of nature spread into the heart and make it eager for life and living.

Spring is upon us. Primroses and violets have already hailed her coming. Rash blooms are showing on the peach trees; the swollen buds of the pear trees and the lilacs point to the blossoming that is to be; the honeysuckles are already green.

27th October 1853. — . . . The center of life is neither in thought nor in feeling, nor in will, nor even in consciousness, so far as it thinks, feels, or wishes. For moral truth may have been penetrated and possessed in all these ways, and escape us still.

Deeper even than consciousness there is our being itself, our very substance, our nature. Only those truths which have entered into this last region, which have become ourselves, become spontaneous and involuntary, instinctive and unconscious, are really our life—that is to something more than our property. So long as we are able to distinguish any space whatever between the truth and us we remain outside it.

The thought, the feeling, the desire, the consciousness of life, are not yet quite life. But peace and repose can nowhere be found except in life and in eternal life, and the eternal life is the divine life, is God. To become divine is then the aim of life: then only can truth be said to be ours beyond the possibility of loss, because it is no longer outside us, nor even in us, but we are it, and it is we; we ourselves are a truth, a will, a work of God. Liberty has become nature; the creature is one with its creator—one through love. It is what it ought to be; its education is finished, and its final happiness begins. The sun of time declines and the light of eternal blessedness arises.

Our fleshly hearts may call this mysticism. It is the mysticism of Jesus: "I am one with the Father; ye shall be one with me. We will be one with you."

17 April 1855. — The weather is still incredible brilliant, warm, and clear. The day is full of the singing of birds, the night is full of stars—Nature has become all kindness, and it is a kindness clothed upon with splendor.

For nearly two hours have I been lost in the contemplation of this magnificent spectacle. I felt myself in the temple of the infinite, in the presence of the worlds, God's guest in this vast nature. The stars wandering in the pale ether drew me far away from earth. What peace beyond the power of words, what dews of life eternal, they shed on the adoring soul! I felt the earth floating like a boat in this blue ocean. Such deep and tranquil delight nourishes the whole man—it purifies and ennobles. I surrendered myself—I was all gratitude and docility.

4th September 1855. — . . . Unity of life, of force, of action, of expression, is becoming impossible to me; I am legion, division, analysis, and reflection; the passion for dialectic, for fine distinctions, absorbs and weakens me. The point which I have reached seems to be explained by a too restless search for perfection, by the abuse of the critical faculty, and by an unreasonable distrust of first impulses, first thoughts, first words. Unity and simplicity of being, confidence, and spontaneity of life, are drifting out of my reach, and this is why I can no longer act.

Give up, then, this trying to know all, to embrace all. Learn to limit yourself, to content yourself with some definite thing, and some definite work; dare to be what you are, and learn to resign with a good grace all that you are not, and to believe in your own individuality. Self-distrust is destroying you; trust, surrender, abandon yourself; "believe and thou shalt be healed." Unbelief is death, and depression and self-satire are alike unbelief.

From the point of view of happiness, the problem of life is insoluble, for it is our highest aspirations which prevent us from being happy. From the point of view of duty, there is the same difficulty, for the fulfillment of duty brings peace, not happiness. It is divine love, the love of the holiest, the possession of God by faith, which solves the difficulty; for if sacrifice has itself become a joy, a lasting, growing and imperishable joy—the soul is then secure of an all-sufficient and unfailing nourishment.

Waking Up Again

from *Attitudes of Gratitude*

M. J. RYAN

Buddhist and Sufi teachers spend a lot of time talking about "waking up," by which they mean, I think, living life to its fullest because we are aware of living it moment to moment. Aware of breathing in, aware of breathing out; aware of chewing and swallowing our food; aware of placing one foot in front of the other when walking. Aware of seeing your infant son, of the effect of your words on coworkers, of the fact that your one foot is resting on top of the other.

Spiritual leaders teach that waking up is a process, that it doesn't just happen once and for all, but must occur again and again when we realize we have forgotten the miracle of being alive, and in recognizing our forgetfulness, we wake to the miracle once again. In the moments we are awake to the wonder of simply being alive, gratitude flows, no matter what our circumstances.

Simplicity and Self-Consciousness

A Letter

FRANÇOIS FÉNELON

There is a simplicity that is merely a fault, and there is a simplicity that is a wonderful virtue. Sometimes it comes from a lack of discernment and an ignorance of what is due others. In the world when people call anyone simple they generally mean a foolish, ignorant, credulous person. But real simplicity, far from being foolish, is almost sublime. All good people like and admire it . . . and yet they could not precisely define it. . . .

I should say that simplicity is an uprightness of soul that prevents self-consciousness. It is not the same as sincerity, which is a much humbler virtue. Many people are sincere who are not simple. They say nothing but what they believe to be true, and do not aim at appearing anything but what they are. But they are continually in fear of passing for something they are not, and so they are forever thinking about themselves, weighing their every word and thought and dwelling upon themselves in fear of having done too much or too little. These people are sincere, but they are not simple. They are not at ease with others, or others with them. There is nothing easy, frank, unrestrained, or natural about them. We feel that we would like less admirable people better, people who are not so stiff! This is how people feel, and God's judgment is the same. He does not like souls that are self-absorbed, and are always, so to speak, looking at themselves in a mirror.

One extreme as opposed to simplicity is to be absorbed in the world around us, never turning a thought within, as is the blind condition of some who are carried away by what is present and tangible. The other extreme is to be self-absorbed in everything, whether it is duty to God or other people, and as a result making us wise in our own conceits—reserved, self-conscious, uneasy at the least thing that disturbs our inward self-complacency. Such false wisdom, in spite of its solemnity, is hardly less vain and foolish than the folly of those who plunge headlong into worldly pleasure. The first are impassioned by their outer surroundings, the others by what they believe themselves to be doing inwardly. But both are in a state of intoxication, and the last is a worse state than the first, because it seems to be wise, though it is not really—and so people do not try to be cured. They rather pride themselves on this state, and feel exalted above others by it. It is a sickness somewhat like insanity—a person may be at death's door while claiming to be well.

Those who are so carried away by outer things that they never look within are in a state of worldly intoxication; and those who dissect themselves continually become affected, and are equally far from being simple.

Real simplicity lies in a happy medium, equally free from thoughtlessness and affectation, in which the soul is not overwhelmed by external things so that it can look within, nor is it given up to the endless introspection that self-consciousness induces. The soul that looks where it is going, without losing time arguing over every step, or looking back perpetually, possesses true simplicity.

Once all self-seeking and brooding is overcome, the soul acquires indescribable peace and freedom. We may write about it, but only experience can really teach anyone what it is. The person who attains it is like a child at its mother's breast, free from fears or longings, ready to be turned this way and that. It is indifferent as to what others may think, except so far as charity always would deliberately avoid scandal. It is always doing everything as well as possible, cheerfully, heartily, but not worried about success or failure. . . .

How far most of us are from real simplicity of heart! Still, the farther we are, the more urgently we should seek it. Far from being simple, the greater number of Christians are not even sincere. They are not merely artificial, but often false and dissimulating toward their neighbors, toward God, and toward themselves. What endless little maneuvers and unrealities and inventions people employ to distort truth! The pity is that [as the psalmist says,] "all men are liars!" . . . Even those who are naturally upright and sincere, whose disposition is what we call frank and simple, are often jealously self-conscious and foster a pride that destroys all real simplicity. Real simplicity consists in genuine forgetfulness of self.

How can you help being constantly self-engrossed when a crowd of anxious thoughts disturbs you and sets you ill at ease? Do only what is in your own power to do! Never voluntarily give way to these disturbing anxieties. If we are steadfast in resisting them whenever we become conscious of their existence, by degrees we will get free. But do not hunt them out with the notion of conquering them! Do not seek a collision—you will only feed the evil. A continual attempt to repress thoughts of self and self-interest is practically continual self-consciousness, which will only distract us from the duties incumbent on us and deprive us of the sense of God's presence.

The great thing is to resign all our interest, pleasures, comfort, and fame to God. Those who unreservedly accept whatever God may give them in this world—humiliation, trouble, and trial from within or without—have made a great step toward self-victory. They will not dread praise or censure. They will not be sensitive. Or, if they find themselves wincing, they will deal so roughly with their own sensitiveness that it will soon die away. Such full resignation and unfeigned acquiescence is true freedom, and from this arises perfect simplicity. The soul that knows no self-seeking, no hidden motives, is thoroughly candid. It goes straight ahead without any hindrance. Its path opens daily more and more to "perfect day." And its peace, amid whatever troubles beset it, will be as boundless as the depths of the sea. But the soul that still seeks self is constrained, hesitating, smothered by the risings of self-love. Blessed indeed are those who are no longer their own, but have given themselves completely to God!

The world takes the same view as God in relation to a noble, self-forgetting simplicity. The world knows how to appreciate among its own worldly people the easy, simple manners of unselfishness, because there is really nothing more beautiful and attractive than a thorough absence of self-consciousness. But this is out of keeping for worldly people. They rarely forget self unless it is when they are altogether absorbed by still more worthless external interests. Yet, even such simplicity of heart as the world can produce gives us some faint idea of the beauty of the real thing. Those who cannot find the substance sometimes run after the shadows, and shadow though it may be, it attracts them for lack of better things.

Take persons who are full of faults, but not seeking to hide them . . ., claiming neither talent, goodness, nor grace, not seeming to think more of themselves than of others, not continually remembering that self to which most of us are so alive. Such persons will be generally liked in spite of many faults. Their spurious simplicity passes as genuine. On the contrary, very clever persons, full of acquired virtues and external gifts, will always be jarring, disagreeable, and repulsive if they seem to be living in perpetual self-consciousness and affectation. So we may safely say that even from the lower point of view, nothing is more attractive or desirable than a simple character free from self-consciousness.

But you will say, am I never to think of myself, or of what affects me? Am I never to speak of myself? No indeed, I would not have you so confined: such an attempt at being simple would destroy all simplicity. What is to be done, then? Make no rules at all, but try to avoid all affectation. When you are disposed to talk about yourself from self-consciousness, thwart the itching desire by quietly turning your attention to God or to some duty that he sets before you.

Remember, simplicity is free from false shame and mock modesty as well as from ostentation and self-conceit. When you feel inclined to talk about yourself out of vanity, the only thing to be done is to stop short as soon as possible. But if, on the other hand, there is some real reason for doing so, then do not perplex yourself with arguments, but go straight to the point. . . .

Such simplicity as this influences all things, including outward manners, and makes people natural and unaffected. You get accustomed to act in a straightforward way, something that is incomprehensible to those who are always self-occupied and artificial. Then even your faults will turn to good, humbling you without depressing you. When God intends to make use of you for his glory, either he will take away your failings or overrule them to his own ends, or at all events, he will so order things that they should not be an obstacle to those among whom he sends you. And practically, those who attain such real inward simplicity generally acquire with it a candid, natural manner, one that may even sometimes appear somewhat too easy and careless, but that will be characterized by a truthful, gentle, innocent, cheerful and calm simplicity, which is exceedingly attractive.

Truly such simplicity is a great treasure!

Not Mere Aestheticism

from *The Book of Tea*

KAKUZO OKAKURA

The Philosophy of Tea is not mere aestheticism in the ordinary acceptance of the term, for it expresses conjointly with ethics and religion our whole point of view about man and nature. It is hygiene, for it enforces cleanliness; it is economics, for it shows comfort in simplicity rather than in the complex and costly; it is moral geometry, inasmuch as it defines our sense of proportion to the universe.

Those of us who know not the secret of properly regulating our own existence on this tumultuous sea of foolish troubles which we call life are constantly in a state of misery while vainly trying to appear happy and contented. We stagger in the attempt to keep our moral equilibrium, and see forerunners of the tempest in every cloud that floats on the horizon. Yet there is joy and beauty in the roll of billows as they sweep outward toward eternity.

Simplicity, Simplicity, Simplicity!

from *Walden*

HENRY DAVID THOREAU

When first I took up my abode in the woods, that is, began to spend my nights as well as days there, which, by accident, was on Independence Day, or the Fourth of July, 1845, my house was not finished for winter, but was merely a defence against the rain, without plastering or chimney, the walls being of rough, weather-stained boards, with wide chinks, which made it cool at night. The upright white hewn studs and freshly planed door and window casings gave it a clean and airy look, especially in the morning, when its timbers were saturated with dew, so that I fancied that by noon some sweet gum would exude from them. To my imagination it retained throughout the day more or less of this auroral character, reminding me of a certain house on a mountain which I had visited a year before. This was an airy and unplastered cabin, fit to entertain a travelling god, and where a goddess might trail her garments. The winds which passed over my dwelling were such as sweep over the ridges of mountains, bearing the broken strains, or celestial parts only, of terrestrial music. The morning wind forever blows, the poem of creation is uninterrupted; but few are the ears that hear it. Olympus is but the outside of the earth everywhere.

The only house I had been the owner of before, if I except a boat, was a tent, which I used occasionally when making excursions in the summer, and this is still rolled up in my garret; but the boat, after passing from hand to hand, has gone down the stream of time. With this more substantial shelter about me, I had made some progress toward settling in the world. This frame, so slightly clad, was a sort of crystallization around me, and reacted on the builder. It was suggestive somewhat as a picture in outlines. I did not need to go outdoors to take the air, for the atmosphere within had lost none of its freshness. It was not so much within doors as behind a door where I sat, even in the rainiest weather. The Harivamsa says, "An abode without birds is like a meat without seasoning." Such was not my abode, for I found myself suddenly neighbor to the birds; not by having imprisoned one, but having caged myself near them. I was not only nearer to some of those which commonly frequent the garden and the orchard, but to those smaller and more thrilling songsters of the forest which never, or rarely, serenade a villager—the wood thrush, the veery, the scarlet tanager, the field sparrow, the whip-poor-will, and many others.

I was seated by the shore of a small pond, about a mile and a half south of the village of Concord and somewhat higher than it, in the midst of an extensive wood between that town and Lincoln, and about two miles south of that our only field known to fame, Concord Battle Ground; but I was so low in the woods that the opposite shore, half a mile off, like the rest, covered with wood, was my most distant horizon. For the first week, whenever I looked out on the pond it impressed me like a tarn high up on the side of a mountain, its bottom far above the surface of other lakes, and, as the sun arose, I saw it throwing off its nightly clothing of mist, and here and there, by degrees, its soft ripples or its smooth reflecting surface was revealed, while the mists, like ghosts, were stealthily withdrawing in every direction into the woods, as at the breaking up of some nocturnal conventicle. The very dew seemed to hang upon the trees later into the day than usual, as on the sides of mountains.

This small lake was of most value as a neighbor in the intervals of a gentle rain-storm in August, when, both air and water being perfectly still, but the sky overcast, mid-afternoon had all the serenity of evening, and the wood thrush sang around, and was heard from shore to shore. A lake like this is never smoother than at such a time; and the clear portion of the air above it being, shallow and darkened by clouds, the water, full of light and reflections, becomes a lower heaven itself so much the more important. From a hill-top near by, where the wood had been recently cut off, there was a pleasing vista southward across the pond, through a wide indentation in the hills which form the shore there, where their opposite sides sloping toward each other suggested a stream flowing out in that direction through a wooded valley, but stream there was none. That way I looked between and over the near green hills to some distant and higher ones in the horizon, tinged with blue. Indeed, by standing on tiptoe I could catch a glimpse of some of the peaks of the still bluer and more distant mountain ranges in the northwest, those true-blue coins from heaven's own mint, and also of some portion of the village. But in other directions, even from this point, I could not see over or beyond the woods which surrounded me. It is well to have some water in your neighborhood, to give buoyancy to and float the earth. One value even of the smallest well is, that when you look into it you see that earth is not continent but insular. This is as important as that it keeps butter cool. When I looked across the pond from this peak toward the Sudbury meadows, which in time of flood I distinguished elevated perhaps by a mirage in their seething valley, like a coin in a basin, all the earth beyond the pond appeared like a thin crust insulated and floated even by this small sheet of interverting water, and I was reminded that this on which I dwelt was but dry land.

Though the view from my door was still more contracted, I did not feel crowded or confined in the least. There was pasture enough for my imagination. The low shrub oak plateau to which the opposite shore arose stretched away toward the prairies of the West and the steppes of Tartary, affording ample room for all the roving families of men. "There are none happy in the world but beings who enjoy freely a vast horizon"—said Damodara, when his herds required new and larger pastures.

Both place and time were changed, and I dwelt nearer to those parts of the universe and to those eras in history which had most attracted me. Where I lived was as far off as many a region viewed nightly by astronomers. We are wont to imagine rare and delectable places in some remote and more celestial corner of the system, behind the constellation of Cassiopeia's Chair, far from noise and disturbance. I discovered that my house actually had its site in such a withdrawn, but forever new and unprofaned, part of the universe. If it were worth the while to settle in those parts near to the Pleiades or the Hyades, to Aldebaran or Altair, then I was really there, or at an equal remoteness from the life which I had left behind, dwindled and twinkling with as fine a ray to my nearest neighbor, and to be seen only in moonless nights by him. Such was that part of creation where I had squatted;

> "There was a shepherd that did live,
>   And held his thoughts as high
> As were the mounts whereon his flocks
>   Did hourly feed him by."

What should we think of the shepherd's life if his flocks always wandered to higher pastures than his thoughts?

Every morning was a cheerful invitation to make my life of equal simplicity, and I may say innocence, with Nature herself. I have been as sincere a worshipper of Aurora as the Greeks. I got up early and bathed in the pond; that was a religious exercise, and one of the best things which I did. They say that characters were engraven on the bathing tub of King Tchingthang to this effect: "Renew thyself completely each day; do it again, and again, and forever again." I can understand that. Morning brings back the heroic ages. I was as much affected by the faint hum of a mosquito making its invisible and unimaginable tour through my apartment at earliest dawn, when I was sitting with door and windows open, as I could be by any trumpet that ever sang of fame. It was Homer's requiem; itself an Iliad and Odyssey in the air, singing its own wrath and wanderings. There was something cosmical about it; a standing advertisement, till forbidden, of the everlasting vigor and fertility of the world.

The morning, which is the most memorable season of the day, is the awakening hour. Then there is least somnolence in us; and for an hour, at least, some part of us awakes which slumbers all the rest of the day and night. Little is to be expected of that day, if it can be called a day, to which we are not awakened by our Genius, but by the mechanical nudgings of some servitor, are not awakened by our own newly acquired force and aspirations from within, accompanied by the undulations of celestial music, instead of factory bells, and a fragrance filling the air—to a higher life than we fell asleep from; and thus the darkness bear its fruit, and prove itself to be good, no less than the light. That man who does not believe that each day contains an earlier, more sacred, and auroral hour than he has yet profaned, has despaired of life, and is pursuing a descending and darkening way. After a partial cessation of his sensuous life, the soul of man, or its organs rather, are reinvigorated each day, and his Genius tries again what noble life it can make.

All memorable events, I should say, transpire in morning time and in a morning atmosphere. The Vedas say, "All intelligences awake with the morning." Poetry and art, and the fairest and most memorable of the actions of men, date from such an hour. All poets and heroes, like Memnon, are the children of Aurora, and emit their music at sunrise. To him whose elastic and vigorous thought keeps pace with the sun, the day is a perpetual morning. It matters not what the clocks say or the attitudes and labors of men. Morning is when I am awake and there is a dawn in me. Moral reform is the effort to throw off sleep. Why is it that men give so poor an account of their day if they have not been slumbering? They are not such poor calculators. If they had not been overcome with drowsiness, they would have performed something. The millions are awake enough for physical labor; but only one in a million is awake enough for effective intellectual exertion, only one in a hundred millions to a poetic or divine life. To be awake is to be alive. I have never yet met a man who was quite awake. How could I have looked him in the face?

We must learn to reawaken and keep ourselves awake, not by mechanical aids, but by an infinite expectation of the dawn, which does not forsake us in our soundest sleep. I know of no more encouraging fact than the unquestionable ability of man to elevate his life by a conscious endeavor. It is something to be able to paint a particular picture, or to carve a statue, and so to make a few objects beautiful; but it is far more glorious to carve and paint the very atmosphere and medium through which we look, which morally we can do. To affect the quality of the day, that is the highest of arts. Every man is tasked to make his life, even in its details, worthy of the contemplation of his most elevated and critical hour. If we refused, or rather used up, such paltry information as we get, the oracles would distinctly inform us how this might be done.

I went to the woods because I wished to live deliberately, to front only the essential facts of life, and see if I could not learn what it had to teach, and not, when I came to die, discover that I had not lived. I did not wish to live what was not life, living is so dear; nor did I wish to practise resignation, unless it was quite necessary. I wanted to live deep and suck out all the marrow of life, to live so sturdily and Spartan-like as to put to rout all that was not life, to cut a broad swath and shave close, to drive life into a corner, and reduce it to its lowest terms, and, if it proved to be mean, why then to get the whole and genuine meanness of it, and publish its meanness to the world; or if it were sublime, to know it by experience, and be able to give a true account of it in my next excursion. For most men, it appears to me, are in a strange uncertainty about it, whether it is of the devil or of God, and have somewhat hastily concluded that it is the chief end of man here to "glorify God and enjoy him forever."

Still we live meanly, like ants; though the fable tells us that we were long ago changed into men; like pygmies we fight with cranes; it is error upon error, and clout upon clout, and our best virtue has for its occasion a superfluous and evitable wretchedness. Our life is frittered away by detail. An honest man has hardly need to count more than his ten fingers, or in extreme cases he may add his ten toes, and lump the rest. Simplicity, simplicity, simplicity! I say, let your affairs be as two or three, and not a hundred or a thousand; instead of a million count half a dozen, and keep your accounts on your thumb-nail. In the midst of this chopping sea of civilized life, such are the clouds and storms and quicksands and thousand-and-one items to be allowed for, that a man has to live, if he would not founder and go to the bottom and not make his port at all, by dead reckoning, and he must be a great calculator indeed who succeeds.

Simplify, simplify. Instead of three meals a day, if it be necessary eat but one; instead of a hundred dishes, five; and reduce other things in proportion. Our life is like a German Confederacy, made up of petty states, with its boundary forever fluctuating, so that even a German cannot tell you how it is bounded at any moment. The nation itself, with all its so-called internal improvements, which, by the way are all external and superficial, is just such an unwieldy and overgrown establishment, cluttered with furniture and tripped up by its own traps, ruined by luxury and heedless expense, by want of calculation and a worthy aim, as the million households in the land; and the only cure for it, as for them, is in a rigid economy, a stern and more than Spartan simplicity of life and elevation of purpose. It lives too fast.

Men think that it is essential that the Nation have commerce, and export ice, and talk through a telegraph, and ride thirty miles an hour, without a doubt, whether they do or not; but whether we should live like baboons or like men, is a little uncertain. If we do not get out sleepers, and forge rails, and devote days and nights to the work, but go to tinkering upon our lives to improve them, who will build railroads? And if railroads are not built, how shall we get to heaven in season? But if we stay at home and mind our business, who will want railroads? We do not ride on the railroad; it rides upon us. . . .

Why should we live with such hurry and waste of life? We are determined to be starved before we are hungry.

Men say that a stitch in time saves nine, and so they take a thousand stitches today to save nine tomorrow. As for work, we haven't any of any consequence. We have the Saint Vitus' dance, and cannot possibly keep our heads still. If I should only give a few pulls at the parish bell-rope, as for a fire, that is, without setting the bell, there is hardly a man on his farm in the outskirts of Concord, notwithstanding that press of engagements which was his excuse so many times this morning, nor a boy, nor a woman, I might almost say, but would forsake all and follow that sound, not mainly to save property from the flames, but, if we will confess the truth, much more to see it burn, since burn it must, and we, be it known, did not set it on fire—or to see it put out, and have a hand in it, if that is done as handsomely; yes, even if it were the parish church itself.

Hardly a man takes a half-hour's nap after dinner, but when he wakes he holds up his head and asks, "What's the news?" as if the rest of mankind had stood his sentinels. Some give directions to be waked every half-hour, doubtless for no other purpose; and then, to pay for it, they tell what they have dreamed. After a night's sleep the news is as indispensable as the breakfast. "Pray tell me anything new that has happened to a man anywhere on this globe"—and he reads it over his coffee and rolls, that a man has had his eyes gouged out this morning on the Wachito River; never dreaming the while that he lives in the dark unfathomed mammoth cave of this world, and has but the rudiment of an eye himself.

For my part, I could easily do without the post-office. I think that there are very few important communications made through it. To speak critically, I never received more than one or two letters in my life—I wrote this some years ago—that were worth the postage. The penny-post is, commonly, an institution through which you seriously offer a man that penny for his thoughts which is so often safely offered in jest.

And I am sure that I never read any memorable news in a newspaper. If we read of one man robbed, or murdered, or killed by accident, or one house burned, or one vessel wrecked, or one steamboat blown up, or one cow run over on the Western Railroad, or one mad dog killed, or one lot of grasshoppers in the winter—we never need read of another. One is enough. If you are acquainted with the principle, what do you care for a myriad instances and applications? To a philosopher all news, as it is called, is gossip, and they who edit and read it are old women over their tea. Yet not a few are greedy after this gossip. There was such a rush, as I hear, the other day at one of the offices to learn the foreign news by the last arrival,

85

that several large squares of plate glass belonging to the establishment were broken by the pressure—news which I seriously think a ready wit might write a twelve-month, or twelve years, beforehand with sufficient accuracy.

As for Spain, for instance, if you know how to throw in Don Carlos and the Infanta, and Don Pedro and Seville and Granada, from time to time in the right proportions—they may have changed the names a little since I saw the papers— and serve up a bull-fight when other entertainments fail, it will be true to the letter, and give us as good an idea of the exact state or ruin of things in Spain as the most succinct and lucid reports under this head in the newspapers: and as for England, almost the last significant scrap of news from that quarter was the revolution of 1649; and if you have learned the history of her crops for an average year, you never need attend to that thing again, unless your speculations are of a merely pecuniary character. If one may judge who rarely looks into the newspapers, nothing new does ever happen in foreign parts, a French revolution not excepted.

What news! how much more important to know what that is which was never old! "Kieou-he-yu (great dignitary of the state of Wei) sent a man to Khoung-tseu to know his news. Khoung-tseu caused the messenger to be seated near him, and questioned him in these terms: What is your master doing? The messenger answered with respect: My master desires to diminish the number of his faults, but he cannot come to the end of them. The messenger being gone, the philosopher remarked: What a worthy messenger! What a worthy messenger!"

The preacher, instead of vexing the ears of drowsy farmers on their day of rest at the end of the week—for Sunday is the fit conclusion of an ill-spent week, and not the fresh and brave beginning of a new one—with this one other draggle-tail of a sermon, should shout with thundering voice, "Pause! Avast! Why so seeming fast, but deadly slow?"

Shams and delusions are esteemed for soundest truths, while reality is fabulous. If men would steadily observe realities only, and not allow themselves to be deluded, life, to compare it with such things as we know, would be like a fairy tale and the Arabian Nights' Entertainments.

If we respected only what is inevitable and has a right to be, music and poetry would resound along the streets. When we are unhurried and wise, we perceive that only great and worthy things have any permanent and absolute existence, that petty fears and petty pleasures are but the shadow of the reality. This is always exhilarating and sublime. By closing the eyes and slumbering, and consenting to be deceived by shows, men establish and confirm their daily life of routine and habit everywhere, which still is built on purely illusory foundations. Children, who play life, discern its true law and relations more clearly than men, who fail to live it worthily, but who think that they are wiser by experience, that is, by failure.

I have read in a Hindoo book, that "There was a king's son, who, being expelled in infancy from his native city, was brought up by a forester, and, growing up to maturity in that state, imagined himself to belong to the barbarous race with which he lived. One of his father's ministers having discovered him, revealed to him what he was, and the misconception of his character was removed, and he knew himself to be a prince. So soul," continues the Hindoo philosopher, "from the circumstances in which it is placed, mistakes its own character, until the truth is revealed to it by some holy teacher, and then it knows itself to be Brahme."

I perceive that we inhabitants of New England live this mean life that we do because our vision does not penetrate the surface of things. We think that that is which appears to be. If a man should walk through this town and see only the reality, where, think you, would the "Mill-dam" go to? If he should give us an account of the realities he beheld there, we should not recognize the place in his description. Look at a meeting-house, or a court-house, or a jail, or a shop, or a dwelling-house, and say what that thing really is before a true gaze, and they would all go to pieces in your account of them. Men esteem truth remote, in the outskirts of the system, behind the farthest star, before Adam and after the last man.

In eternity there is indeed something true and sublime. But all these times and places and occasions are now and here. God himself culminates in the present moment, and will never be more divine in the lapse of all the ages. And we are enabled to apprehend at all what is sublime and noble only by the perpetual instilling and drenching of the reality that surrounds us. The universe constantly and obediently answers to our conceptions; whether we travel fast or slow, the track is laid for us. Let us spend our lives in conceiving then. The poet or the artist never yet had so fair and noble a design but some of his posterity at least could accomplish it.

Let us spend one day as deliberately as Nature, and not be thrown off the track by every nutshell and mosquito's wing that falls on the rails. Let us rise early and fast, or break fast, gently and without perturbation; let company come and let company go, let the bells ring and the children cry—determined to make a day of it. Why should we knock under and go with the stream? Let us not be upset and overwhelmed in that terrible rapid and whirlpool called a dinner, situated in the meridian shallows. Weather this danger and you are safe, for the rest of the way is down hill. With unrelaxed nerves, with morning vigor, sail by it, looking another way, tied to the mast like Ulysses. If the engine whistles, let it whistle till it is hoarse for its pains. If the bell rings, why should we run? We will consider what kind of music they are like.

Let us settle ourselves, and work and wedge our feet downward through the mud and slush of opinion, and prejudice, and tradition, and delusion, and appearance, that alluvion which covers the globe, through Paris and London, through New York and Boston and Concord, through Church and State, through poetry and philosophy and religion, till we come to a hard bottom and rocks in place, which we can call reality, and say, This is, and no mistake; and then begin, having a point d'appui, below freshet and frost and fire, a place where you might found a wall or a state, or set a lamp-post safely, or perhaps a gauge, not a Nilometer, but a Realometer, that future ages might know how deep a freshet of shams and appearances had gathered from time to time. If you stand right fronting and face to face to a fact, you will see the sun glimmer on both its surfaces, as if it were a cimeter, and feel its sweet edge dividing you through the heart and marrow, and so you will happily conclude your mortal career. Be it life or death, we crave only reality. If we are really dying, let us hear the rattle in our throats and feel cold in the extremities; if we are alive, let us go about our business.

Time is but the stream I go a-fishing in. I drink at it; but while I drink I see the sandy bottom and detect how shallow it is. Its thin current slides away, but eternity remains. I would drink deeper; fish in the sky, whose bottom is pebbly with stars. I cannot count one. I know not the first letter of the alphabet. I have always been regretting that I was not as wise as the day I was born. The intellect is a cleaver; it discerns and rifts its way into the secret of things. I do not wish to be any more busy with my hands than is necessary. My head is hands and feet. I feel all my best faculties concentrated in it. My instinct tells me that my head is an organ for burrowing, as some creatures use their snout and fore paws, and with it I would mine and burrow my way through these hills. I think that the richest vein is somewhere hereabouts; so by the divining-rod and thin rising vapors I judge; and here I will begin to mine.

Closing Prayers

I pray that out of his glorious riches he may strengthen you with power through his Spirit in your inner being, so that Christ may dwell in your hearts through faith. And I pray that you, being rooted and established in love, may have power, together with all the Lord's holy people, to grasp how wide and long and high and deep is the love of Christ, and to know this love that surpasses knowledge—that you may be filled to the measure of all the fullness of God.

—EPHESIANS 3:16–19 (NIV)

You are the peace of all things calm

You are the place to hide from harm

You are the light that shines in dark

You are the heart's eternal spark

You are the door that's open wide

You are the guest who waits inside

You are the stranger at the door

You are the calling of the poor

You are my Lord and with me still

You are my love, keep me from ill

You are the light, the truth, the way

You are my Savior this very day.

—FIRST-MILLENNIUM CELTIC PRAYER

And let the peace of Christ rule in your hearts,
to which indeed you were called in the one body.
And be thankful.

—COLOSSIANS 3:15

Sources

Amiel, Henri-Frédéric. *Amiel's Journal: The Journal Intime of Henri-Frédéric Amiel*, Second Edition, translated by Mrs. Humphrey Ward. London: Macmillan and Co., 1889: 12–3, 51–52.

Bourgeault, Cynthia. *Centering Prayer and Inner Awakening*. Lanham, MD: Cowley Pub., 2004: 132.

Hanh, Thich Nhat. *Living Buddha, Living Christ*. New York: Riverhead Books, 1995: 14.

Jewett, Sarah Orne. *The Country of the Pointed Firs*. Boston: Houghton Mifflin, 1910: 221–223.

Kempis, Thomas à. Adapted to modern English from *The Imitation of Christ in Three Books*, translated by John Payne. London: J.F. Dove, 1820: 101.

Markova, Dawna. *I Will Not Die an Unlived Life: Reclaiming Purpose and Passion*. Berkeley, CA: Conari Press, 2000: 17–18.

Okakura, Kakuzo. *The Book of Tea*. New York: Fox Duffield & Company, 1906: 3–4, 155–156.

Ryan, M. J. *Attitudes of Gratitude: How to Give and Receive Joy Every Day of Your Life, 10th Anniversary Edition*. San Francisco: Red Wheel/Weiser, 2009: 75–76.

Thoreau, Henry David. *Walden; or, Life in the Woods*. Boston: Ticknor and Fields, 1854: 92–107.

About Paraclete Press

WHO WE ARE

Paraclete Press is a publisher of books, recordings, and DVDs on Christian spirituality. Our publishing represents a full expression of Christian belief and practice—from Catholic to Evangelical, from Protestant to Orthodox.

We are the publishing arm of the Community of Jesus, an ecumenical monastic community in the Benedictine tradition. As such, we are uniquely positioned in the marketplace without connection to a large corporation and with informal relationships to many branches and denominations of faith.

WHAT WE ARE DOING

PARACLETE PRESS BOOKS

Paraclete publishes books that show the richness and depth of what it means to be Christian. Although Benedictine spirituality is at the heart of who we are and all that we do, we publish books that reflect the Christian experience across many cultures, time periods, and houses of worship. We publish books that nourish the vibrant life of the church and its people.

We have several different series, including the best-selling Paraclete Essentials and Paraclete Giants series of classic texts in contemporary English; Voices from the Monastery—men and women monastics writing about living a spiritual life today; our award-winning Paraclete Poetry series as well as the Mount Tabor Books on the arts; best-selling gift books for children on the occasions of baptism and first communion; and the Active Prayer Series that brings creativity and liveliness to any life of prayer.

MOUNT TABOR BOOKS

Paraclete's newest series, Mount Tabor Books, focuses on the arts and literature as well as liturgical worship and spirituality, and was created in conjunction with the Mount Tabor Ecumenical Centre for Art and Spirituality in Barga, Italy.

PARACLETE RECORDINGS

From Gregorian chant to contemporary American choral works, our recordings celebrate the best of sacred choral music composed through the centuries that create a space for heaven and earth to intersect. Paraclete Recordings is the record label representing the internationally acclaimed choir Gloriæ Dei Cantores, praised for their "rapt and fathomless spiritual intensity" by *American Record Guide*; the Gloriæ Dei Cantores Schola, specializing in the study and performance of Gregorian chant; and the other instrumental artists of the Arts Empowering Life Foundation.

Paraclete Press is also privileged to be the exclusive North American distributor of the recordings of the Monastic Choir of St. Peter's Abbey in Solesmes, France, long considered to be a leading authority on Gregorian chant.

PARACLETE VIDEO

Our DVDs offer spiritual help, healing, and biblical guidance for a broad range of life issues including grief and loss, marriage, forgiveness, facing death, bullying, addictions, Alzheimer's, and spiritual formation.

Learn more about us at our website:
www.paracletepress.com, or
call us toll-free at 1-800-451-5006.

SCAN
TO
READ
MORE

You may also be interested in…

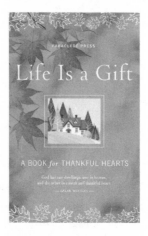

Life is a Gift
A Book for Thankful Hearts

ISBN: 978-1-61261-412-0, $16.99

There is an old proverb from Eastern Europe that says, "Who does not thank for little, will not thank for much." In other words, the person who goes through life being thankful for God's gifts and blessings usually experiences more of life's goodness—and inhabits more of God's blessings. This beautiful book challenges people to live in a way that blesses God, from whom all good things come. Reflections from a wide array of authors are included: Henry van Dyke, Abraham Lincoln, and Louisa May Alcott, as well as many songs, psalms, and prayers.